Other Helen Exley Giftbooks:
To Day (you poor old wreck)
To Mum (the kindest of ladies)
Thoughts on... Being Happy
Words on Joy
Words of Wisdom

Published simultaneously in 1998 by Exley Publications Ltd in
Great Britain, and Exley Publications LLC in the USA.
Copyright © Helen Exley 1998
The moral right of the author has been asserted.

12   11   10   9   8   7   6   5   4   3   2   1

Edited and pictures selected by Helen Exley
ISBN 1-86187-104-X

Printed in Hungary.

**Exley Publications Ltd, 16 Chalk Hill, Watford,
Herts WD1 4BN, UK.
Exley Publications LLC, 232 Madison Avenue,
Suite 1206, NY 10016, USA.**

I WISH YOU HAPPINESS

EDITED BY HELEN EXLEY

EXLEY
NEW YORK • WATFORD, UK

The happy ones
see only beautiful
things

JEREMY LATIMER, 10

SHARON BARRIBALL, 4

THE HAPPY ONES

Some people have a beautiful smile and when people see it they feel happy.

SUSANNAH MORRIS, 10

HAPPINESS IS A DISEASE THAT GROWS ON YOU SOME PEOPLE MORE THAN OTHERS

STEPHEN BATTY

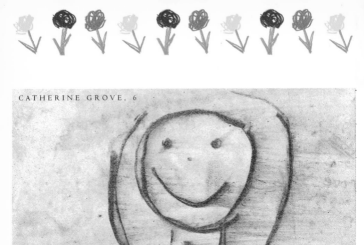

CATHERINE GROVE, 6

A WARM FEELING

Happiness is a warm feeling in your tummy.

TRACEY DOWSON, 8

Happiness makes my heart feel soft.

HARINDER PUREWAL, 10

When I feel so happy I jump to touch
the sky,
When I feel so happy I climb a
mountainside,
When I feel so happy I run around the
world.

ANDREW MOSS, 10

GENTLE PEACE

Happiness is to seek and find peace of mind.

GILLIAN HUGHES, 11

It's the scent of the roses that
fills the air,
And the whispering wind blowing
through my hair.
It's the sparkling dew drops on the ground,
And the gurgling stream that makes hardly
a sound.
It's the feel of the snowflakes that melt
on my tongue.
And the night owl calling to her young.

ELIZABETH ANNE DE GREY

MARK GOODSIR, 11

Happiness is a forest
with scarcely a sound
but bluebells growing
everywhere. GAYNOR CHALLINGSWORTH, 10

THE WORLD IS ALIVE

If flowers had faces they would be smiling
to make everyone happy and trees would be
waving their leaves about to make a breeze.
Then how nice the world would be.

JULIE MARSH, 7

I wish the hills were full of music and
everybody sang. Happy hours we'd spend
in the sun filled days.

MORWENNA POND, 8

I am happy
because the birds
sing to me.

JOSEPHINE, 6

SIMON ANDREWS, 6

Happiness is the breaking of a summer morning.

KIM MILLER, 10

Beauty is the flowers
opening their faces.
Beauty is the larks gliding
over dark blue clouds.
Beauty is the moonlight
creeping up behind huge
mountains.
Beauty is for plants
growing higher, higher,
and higher.
Beauty is for the
wilderness that God has
given us.

MANDY GIBSON, 10

GRUMBLES

Sadness is running four hundred yards for a bus when you have forgotten your fare.

D. WHINES, 14

Unhappiness is... finding your sister still alive after eating your homemade pies.

EUGENE MONAGHAN, 14

When you're happy
you look nice,
When your sad
you look horrible.

LYNN SINGLETON, 10

MR. GLUM.

ADRIAN COX, 10

FEELING FREE!

Happiness is the sun in the sky
Galloping on the beach,
Water splashing, feeling free.

MEGHAN SIMMONS, 11

Whenever I've got time to go
somewhere I feel happy. I am free to
go wherever I want. Nobody fussing
around me. I'm free as a bird. You
can't be happy if you're not free.

KEVIN WILLIAMS, 9

Happiness is riding
Happiness is free
Happiness is jumping
So it must be me!

ANDREW TROWBRIDGE, 7

Be
HAPPY
Be
FRee

ZARYK GLASSON, 7

Happiness is
If you give
It a way

When you give someone a
present you feel Well I don't
no really But you feel very
good. Like this year I bought
my mom some scent and
my dad a pair of pants
and I felt Well I don't know
what to say really.

KAREN THOMSON, 5

CLARA FLEMMING, 7

GIVING

Happiness is... getting the
Sixpence in the christmas pud
and giving it to your sister
for her birthday
the next day.

SARAH JANE SIBLEY, 14

Happiness is giving
a little and taking a little, even if it is a mere
dandelion. It is worth a bouquet of red roses
wrapped in delicate lace if it is given with care.

HELEN CADDICK, 11

I like to see the persons face light up with joy,
and the rustling of the wrapping paper
being torn off of the present. It's so nice
when they thank you for the present, and that
warms you all over.

PAUL OWEN, 13

When someone
is unhappy, it is like
a dark shadow cast
over the
world

SOPHIE BERGE, 12

Some items of news are happy. Others are so sad we just can't think of them. It hurts in our minds.

KEVIN WILLIAMS, 9

Sadness is when your mummy and daddy lose their jobs.

PAUL BRADBURN, 8

Sadness is betraying someone.

ALISON WILLIAMS, 12

Sadness is when mammy leave their children.

SHARON HEAP, 7

KERAN HARVEY, 8

SAD AND ALONE

Unhappiness is so unhappy that you feel that you are a cat that is lost.

KAREN LLOYD, 10

JANET BUCKLE, 11

Unhappiness is loosing all your friends,
and not knowing how to make new ones.
When they just run off and play together,
while you stand shivering in the bitter cold.

RICHARD TREMAYNE

It was playtime and there was two very miserable people. They were Janet and me. I thought for a moment and then went over to Janet and tried to be friendly. It was not normal for me to make a friend so soon. But I suppose it was just because I wanted to make someone happy, really I was doing two for the price of one, for when I am making someone happy I am making me happy.

JANE TODD, 10

CATHERINE BAKER, 9

MICHAEL POWELL, 10

If I could have anything in the world I would choose friends.

DAVID JONES, 10

Happiness is my friend's hand.

GILLIAN QUEEN, 10

Happiness is just being with and sharing.

CHERYL O'MALLEY, 10

Happy is the whole world
as friends. It's light all
through your life.

DANIEL DILLING, 8

MY FAMILY

I am happy. Because I am loved.

C. WARMOLL

Happiness is feeling the security of a happy home.

SUSAN THREADINGHAM, 14

Happ

the

Happiness is going home to
a laughing mum.

PETER LEONARD, 7

Happiness is the feeling which wraps itself
around a family. There is a sense of
togetherness which is almost tangible in
the warm atmosphere of the room.

SUSIE GREENAWAY, 14

iness is
ringing up
Grandma on
telephone

CLIVE BATEMAN, 9

GEE! WOW!

The things that make me happy are
flowers dimonds and butterflys and
ladybirds all things that are coloured
and clowns make me laughe and the sun
and summer and the snow makes me
happy and toys makes me and sweets and
the hedgehogs are nice althow they are
prickly and I think everything makes
St. Valantine very happy indeed and trees
make me happy and sheep and cow's and
goates and I like the birds and it makes
me laughe when I see peple with arrows
through there ears and I like the rainbow
and the lightness and I like the stars and
the moon and I like the fields and I like
neklises and braselits.

ELIZABETH WRIGHT

MARTIN CHILDS, 10

JAMIESON SIMEON 6

Happiness is the smell of the air on summer mornings cool and crisp.

LEE WALKER, 8

Happiness is Spring, the small shoots
pushing through the soil, and the baby
birds taking their first flight.

Happiness is Summer, laying in the
sun and forgetting your worries, when
the insects are buzzing amongst the
flowers.

Happiness is Autumn, walking in the
falling crunchy leaves.
Happiness is Winter, speeding a hillside
on a sledge with the wind rushing past
you, and the snow falling softly covering
everything.

SAMANTHA JONES, 11

When the clouds
are floating by,
And the day
goes by and
by. We should
all be smiling;
Not stuck in
a office filing.

M. GURR, 10

SARAH HINKLY, 7

HAPPINESS DOMINATES DISASTER

Happiness is a thing of care and
consideration, it's everywhere.
The birds and the bees show happiness
to the trees.
The sea and the water show care to the
creatures in it.
Happiness dominates disaster.
It glooms away the sorrows which hang
among swallows.
Happiness just comes and goes like the
wild things.
It's gone now but it will be back.

J. QUINNEY

Happiness is to see children from all over
the world playing together like children
from England and Germany and from
countries which have had a war and are
now friends again.

KATHRYN LUKE, 10

ALAN YOUNG, 6

My best moment is when old ladies are being looked after.

SHIRLEY PEAT, 10

JULIE MILLS, 9

To make me happy I would like make other people happy. I want to be nice and to help people.
I want to enjoy every minute of my life by helping all the people in the world when they are poorly.

LISA STANLEY, 7

I don't care if I'm sitting in hell as long as other people are happy. I don't care if I'm starving as long as other people are eating.
I don't care if I'm dying as long as other people are healing.

HELEN CAMERON, 10

It costs nothing to smile at a stranger,
It costs nothing to be happy.
So go on and spread some around.

JEANETTE ACHILLES, 15

LOVED AND CARED FOR

You can't buy things to make you happy. You can't go into a shop and say. Please will you sell me a loving mummy?

MICHELLE BUNNEY, 8

Happiness is a kind of love. You may think that happiness is just getting things but it isn't really.

SHARON MCNEIL, 11

Happiness is when I was in the Orphanage and I saw my Mum.

WAYNE CURZON, 9

Happiness is... being looked after and spoilt

NICOLA BLAIR, 10

Happiness, Happiness you touched my small head.

KEMA AKOMA-MORDI, 10

NICOLA SLEEP, 10

BEYOND ALL TIME

Happiness is peace and freedom,
Deep down in our hearts,
The joy of little childish games,
And jokes and pranks and laughs.
Happiness is little things,
We treasure in our hearts,
To keep them locked and
sealed forever,
until the day we part.

CLARE SOUTHWELL, 12

Happiness is meant for everyone
But is elusive as a butterfly.
Happiness is beautiful,
as a flower.
It cannot be expressed in any rhyme.
It may only last a fraction of an hour.
But it stays inside the heart
beyond all time.

E. WRIGHT

Try to please to love
and care and forgive
will you?

Good. Well so I will
not have to tell you
again, all right.

Right I love you all
Bye.

KIRSTY MEADOWS, 8½

ROWENA LESTER, 5